WRITIN(

CW01024739

Q

ISBN: 978-1-913642-35-8

The author has asserted their right to be identified as the author of this Work in accordance with the Copyright, Designs and Patents Act 1988

Book designed by Aaron Kent

Edited by Aaron Kent

Broken Sleep Books (2021), Talgarreg, Wales

Contents

In arrival, feet flutter like dying birds	7
Contamination	8
Foreigners	9
My mother the philosopher	10
Mother	11
He	12
Invasion	13
Attachment	14
Thresholds	15
Anthropologists	17
Function of inhabiting	18
The dinghy	19
Past tense	20
Non-arrival	22
If this is my face, so be it	23
At the feast of asylum	26
Fingerprinting	43
Her name	44
My mother's feet	45
The camp – is it possible?	46
Photographs	48
Single life	49
A soliloquy before time	50
Time	51
Writing the camp	59
Refugees are dialectical beings	61
The camp is time	66
The camp is the reject of the reject par excellence	68
In mourning the refugee, we mourn God's intention in the absolute	70
A sudden utterance is the stranger	72
Confessions	74
What remains of the camp when the name dies?	76
There it is: the camp that is yet to be born	82
Necessarily, the camp is the border	83

Flesh when mutilated called God   86
The bomb shelter   92
A fistful of solitude   96
Is it distance or is it a far god?   97
An infinite outing; or the cemetery   104
Sensitivity   107
Imbalance   108
Seeing   109
Dialects   110
Face   111
The throne   112
It is a camp despite the name   113
With a third eye, I see the catastrophe   114

Acknowledgements   117

Writing The Camp

Yousif M. Qasmiyeh

For Mustafa
1943-2020

In arrival, feet flutter like dying birds

We think, sometimes,
That they came from countless directions,
From dim-coloured borders,
From the raging fire that devoured them in the beginning,
From absence.
Here they come again, so invite them over to our death.

The refugee is the revenant of the face.

O refugee, feast upon the other to eat yourself.

In arrival, feet flutter like dying birds.

In the camp, time died so it could return home.

Contamination

They told me that my dialect is not as pure as it should be. According to them, I have failed to preserve what I have inherited. But in truth I have inherited nothing. I just heard noises and without even knowing how or why, I accumulated some in my pockets and ran away. I robbed them in daylight.

They tried to catch me but before laying their pure noises on me, I swallowed what became mine quickly.

As I walk on my own, I think of what I swallowed that day. I smile without letting my dialect know that I still do not know what it might sound like in the singular.

Foreigners

I live in Baddawi Camp.

This is what I used to tell foreigners whenever they came to my primary school.

At times I used to run after them and repeat these words without waiting for their questions.

I have always thought that questions are inherent within the answers and that answers very often comprise their questions, questions which no answers can address.

My mother the philosopher

I have always wanted to deputise my mother in my conversations or even present her as a philosopher whose philosophical reflections should not be taken lightly or listened to transiently.

The aim has always been to guide myself, at the expense of my mother, into a place where only people with loud voices are allowed to exist.

The voice was completely mine but the echo was always hers.

I needed her to bring me to the surface, to the realm of being as my mother who enjoyed doing so without questioning my intentions.

From trying to teach her how to write her name into transforming her into a benign philosophical voice, the distance is vast but hers, nonetheless.

Mother

She will die soon
Unless she has already
Without telling me

This is how she normally dies
Discreetly and alone.

He

His parents had survived the holocaust.

When I arrived in Oxford he gave me a scarf (his scarf) and a jumper (his jumper). A week later, I cooked for him with his own ingredients.

Invasion

In their dreams they used to talk with butterflies.

Those who descended into the camp did not like that.

They made sure these people never woke again.

Attachment

Wherever she went I went with her.

I once hid underneath her hanging dress thinking that she might not notice me.

Thresholds

Thresholds embody a polite and, to a certain degree, diluted strategy to appropriate more land without vocally unsettling the socio-political codes of conduct.

Such land-relatedness becomes even more complex when it takes place in refugee camps.

I remember when my father decided to construct the first threshold to our house, announcing that refugees' ability to acquaint and reacquaint themselves with spatial invalidity is the nerve which sustains the normality which is so urgently needed to create a meaningful form of survival and competitiveness.

By doing so, my father's, and other people's, benign attempts to maintain a possessive understanding of well-being have directly contributed to the dramatisation of fossilised life in the camps.

A solid place or a conspicuous marker for residents and foreigners alike to visit whenever they feel like it; a place which suddenly becomes more central in our existence than the house or home itself.

For whom are these thresholds created?

For the people of the house who also become the people of the threshold.

They regularly cross it to access what is deemed more private.

The visitors who, every time they walk towards the door, are sacrificed at the builder's doorstep.

They enter the place through a ceremony that only exists to baptise the feet of the descending crowds.

O crowds, move more slowly so we can all make it to paradise.

O crowds of the hidden, take some air before you delve deeply into the corridors of the sudden.

Our threshold shall not die.

It shall always be there for the enterers, the exiters and above all the escapees.

Blessed is the stone of men and beasts!

Anthropologists

I know some of them.

Some of them are friends but the majority are enemies.

Upon the doorstep you observe what they observe with a lot of care.

You look at them the way they look at you, curiously and obliquely.

You suddenly develop a fear of imitating them whilst they imitate you.

You worry about relapsing into one of your minds while sharing mundane details with them.

Sometimes I dream of devouring all of them, and just once with no witnesses or written testimonies.

All of us wanted to greet her.

Even my illiterate mother who never spoke a word of English said: Welcome!

After spending hours with us, in the same room, she left with a jar of homemade pickles and three full cassettes with our voices.

Function of inhabiting

Even though we tend to have a subtly precarious relationship with our place, we opt to dilute such precariousness, or at least pretend that it does not exist, in order to claim 'the our' in such a linkage; as if it is the place which governs the way we perceive it rather than an independent perception that slowly develops as the act of inhabiting goes on.

We ultimately focus on place as a property and not as a medium where connections, loyalties and sometimes relationships are challenged, deconstructed and eventually reconceptualised.

Thus we inhabit *a place* but there is never sufficient intimacy to inhabit *the place*.

We inhabit it with the ghosts of the before and the after, so we only exist in that bracketed state between what happened and what ought to happen.

My trips from one camp to another were the necessary exercises that I wanted to complete to come to terms with what we might call intimate clumsiness.

I assume that I know them given our shared heritage and yet I hardly know them since they are different. Viewing these differences as present would enable me to extract commonalities by noticing differences more.

The more I add or subtract, the more numbers or features I commit to memory.

Camps only stay the same when we fail to notice them.

The dinghy

When the dinghy started to sink, nobody knew what to do.

Instead they sat motionless, praying to the sun and other things.

I knew one of them.

We met in Manchester.

When we last spoke on the phone, after his asylum claim was rejected, he sounded very down.

Past tense

They asked him to strip off all of his clothes while discussing his asylum claim.

The uniform was loose on him – two sizes bigger to accommodate his solitude.

The being is being strangled somewhere nearby.

On their way to court they disposed of him and his documents.

He never paid any attention to numbers.

They called it his room so he could commit suicide in private.

The last time they called his name he was not there.

His shoes had new soles.

He enjoyed photographing feet, including his own.

His title was written in bold.

His name looked faint.

The interviewer failed to conjugate a verb in the past tense.

He opted for the present tense instead.

He saw *term*, *term*inate and *term*inal on the same page.

He landed unscathed.

His only injury was mental.

In the end, he claimed asylum.

Non-arrival

The moment I arrive, I want to come back.

I never knew why reaching a place has always meant the end of my place.

Whether I walk, travel by bus or train, or fly, I would only be there to mark the occasion of coming back.

Non-arrival, I suppose, can also be another occasion.

If this is my face, so be it

Walking alongside his shadow, he suddenly realised that it was both of them who needed to cross the border.

They fortified their walls with cement and nails. They moved their women and children to a safe place and shouted: They are coming after our faces; they are coming after our crops!

Immemorial is the smell of refugees.

The equivalence of a refugee would be his body.

Wake! He said to his body when they arrived. A bit of air was in the air.

The child has become water... It is to the side, a tad clear, a tad not, but when you look him in the eye you will see the meaning of water.

Whoever can sense the coming is a refugee. The refugee can neither come nor depart; he is the God of gestures.

We might also say: The face is a dead God.

Whoever claims asylum, whoever lends his hands to his strangers so they could bear out his presence and his things, is the one who has many deities and none.

Refugees and gods always compete for the same space.

What is intimate is the face and never the refugee.

The refugee is only intimate in his death and if there is only one death to ponder, it is that of the refugee.

If this is my face, so be it. For once, it is a stone's throw away.

A being with cracked soles is Man.

The refugee is the superimposed being. Not only does he act as an alibi to existence, he also creates existence. Without the refugee, existence is no longer existent.

Refugees, to kill time, count their dead.

Killing time is the correlative to killing themselves.

A no-place is what substantiates a deceased refugee.

A death with no place can never happen.

A refugee only returns to bear witness to his own return.

In the absence of time, arrival takes place.

Claiming asylum always results in the overreading of the proper noun.

This happens when it is enough to say that it is the body that claims asylum. The body by itself. The body as its body. Whatever state it is in, it is the body, the body in the flesh, that submits itself in front of other bodies, in order, first and foremost, to be declared present, made present, or to be seen as such by those with more mature flesh and finer cuts. In the flesh, the refugee arrives while bearing witness to his own body, while holding the narrative of the body: I am sacrificing my body for myself; nobody and nothing else, to edge back into the ladder of bodies and be a sign amidst signs. The body is by itself; bare, melancholic as the body in its first outing. Whatever state it is in, it is that that carries all states to the threshold. To the borderline whose remnant is a body and whose body is a remnant. In the flesh is what the refugee can see with or without the gaze.

Only those who have never seen a place can describe the place.

Those who flee their homes tend to have faces that are slightly clearer than the moon. In the above clarity, only the face can substitute its creator.

In asylum, we borrow our bodies for the last time.

Whenever my mother wanted to leave the house, it was to see God's face. God's face, according to her, was somewhere else.

Man, how is it that your body is intact?

The refugee is he who fears himself. When the self is deafeningly mauled, he will fear the place but never the animal.

There is nothing sacred about the sacred save the eyes.

On the threshold, they slaughtered us and time.

At the feast of asylum

I

In a container to the unknown, or to a place, somewhere and nowhere at the same time, where would-be refugees are kept or are keeping themselves, where they can barely breathe, there is only one time; a series of knotted nothingness that repeats itself for the sake of monotony, but also for the sole reason of unsettling that monotony itself and reclaiming air.

These inhabitants travel with one necessary objective: getting out.

During this horizontal journey new possibilities start to emerge: How would a language, or languages, resurrect the self, or the selves, in a medium where silence - not the absence of speech - is the main composite; how do impermanent tribes and alliances which are formed in situ endure time?

The people are here, en route to somewhere else without knowing the new place.

To realise that they have arrived, they have to believe in something. Would this something be their new religion, the one of innumerable followers and infinite books?

At least they will believe their feet as they hit the ground. The feet might be swollen, but with the same capacity - as the previous ones - to doubt the arrival.

As the lorry moves, they stay motionless and unmoved.

They, with the exception of the frail, might move in their thoughts towards a clearly set and drawn target, that of people who know they are different in the way they measure time and water.

II

Is there a refugee time, an indefinite state of being which is supposedly marked, amongst other things, by an absolute form of recognition and/or forgetfulness for those who are called refugees, a form with unidentifiable ends or conclusions?

I am present *in order to be* recognised, *in order to be* forgotten, and left on my own to gather the very fine details of the flight that is about to commence; this time inwardly, with no exterior or motifs that may be used to retrace our footsteps.

The flight will resume, as if it had never ended, in a direction that would propel the present and the past into one being, that of disappearance, the new undiscovered land.

Then, and only then, would the present become a fluid present while the past, which is mainly governed by what I will say in the present, would be a semi-distant past of faces, pictures and smells.

The semi-distant is not distant at all, but a statement of an order that is desperately needed so I can continue.

But how could this disappearance be reached in the first place? How would an absence - with the bare minimum of a body - be evaluated and sensed?

This might lead us to presume that the journey is that of a being whose main objective is never to arrive.

And yet this non-arrival does not cancel out the place or the point of reference which, if it were to act as an intimate place, has to be imagined as a past with images that continue to depict and sustain the past itself as such.

From now on, the being journeys towards what it desires during that time, not via an entirely permanent desire, but through a medium that becomes welcoming of a being whose movement is only for the sake of imagining, that is, to imagine while seeing with its own eyes.

The being will keep its attention free of subsidiary engagements, for a clear reading of what is about to happen as soon as its feet hit the ground.

But is it a flight after all? We might say 'yes'.

The flight becomes an attempt to live the time that is passing and the one that is fast approaching from all directions.

The flight is taking place only to remind us of the dead, to unite us with the sacred and the profane simultaneously, to unsettle the equilibrium that possesses us and eventually to send us to ourselves wherever we are.

I will land soon. I will land eventually but my time is only different from yours as a sign of difference.

If you accept me, I will accept you.

Not knowing what is about to happen is crucial for the imaginer whose heart never stops beating and whose words, with the help of their time, will start to carry some weight.

Those would be the ones that the being should observe without allowing itself to change the changed, but, instead, to re-gather the particles of its time, this time, that will start to roam the place before it.

Summoning these moments will mark a form of dictatorial time: here I contain what I see as mine without asking about those on the verge of non-arrival.

Time is running away from me in a direction that is not mine.

It is a time with an insatiable sense of place: what we feel is rapidly turning into clouds above our frail bodies and hearts, clouds that can only give birth to nothingness.

In the morning, as at other times, we shall resume our ascension until we reach that land.

We will gather first in that spot that all of us know, but none of us can name, for it is forbidden, according to the norms of journeying, to see each other clearly as we are about to depart.

This time we will need to remember that sooner or later somebody, a stranger like us, will wake us from our deep sleep to inject the time that will happen in our eyes.

Now, the eyes are for the seer whereas the vision is solely for the stranger, the guardian of the land's keys.

I am treading on the time that is raging under my feet to feel what the strangers have left for themselves and others.

They left their time somewhere safe: where beasts gather to share their hunt.

III

Let us eat nothing so we can continue living in normality.

There, over there, and therein, we accept to share these remnants as long as we see what we are sharing.

We dip so deep to cast out the air that has been trapped in our lungs so we can dip again without air.

We smell ourselves and what we still have of the edible in ourselves to pass time and recognise the normal in us.

We then lament the disappearance of the things we used to have and, for once, we think we do not have stomachs.

'Where is our body?' we ask while imagining a broken moon, with its deafening bang, falling somewhere in the vicinity of the body.

Where are our eyes to see what we have done to ourselves and to see how much life is left in us.

We eat ourselves and when we are about to die we eat each other.

IV

The queue outside was infinitely long. I was there and so were my brothers in asylum. As we reached the main gate, they started ushering us in, one after the other.

The queue remained in our absence.

We handed them our hands, printed our names and left the Reporting Centre thinking that we may have found the real God, the one who never shrinks.

V

In groups, together, one after the other, next to each other, we walk, for it is walking that we shall remember. It is, after all, our only memory.

VI

In the end they decided not to ask him any further questions. They left him to his tears and descended one after the other with minimal noise.

VII

He is my friend. The person who allowed me to be his friend when we first met at the bus-stop. When they asked me to leave the city he invited me to his place and handed me his key. 'Here, you are going to live with me in this room', he said. 'But is there space for me in the presence of all these people?' I asked, while counting the flat bodies in the small room. And with the stretch of a hand he shoved the mound of shoes to one side and said: 'Exactly here, by the doorstep, will be your place.'

VIII

You are the stranger, the one who does not have an equal, for it is a sin to be like them or to forge a path with those who are still on the road, like you. They said: Stay away, O stranger, from our crops and beasts and if it happens that you make it to our land, be the one whose smell does not reach our air, be the mad one.

IX

It is when absence meets absence, when blindness sees blindness from a distance without recognising itself, and when that which is coming our way stops to catch its breath so we can catch ours, then, and only then, will a good death happen.

X

Dying also includes the death of what we thought we knew,

the embattled sounds under our skin and above,

the mornings we wrongly accused of betraying our solitude,

the notes we left in various corners of the house –

corners that we might stumble upon when death is
complete.

XI

It is like being yourself, but with a self that is hardly there to accompany you on this journey.

Everything; precisely, everything that is there, is dead or dying. The people, my people, are all dead even if they, for whatever reason, think otherwise. The plants, their plants, which now look alive, will die very soon.

When I entered the house, this time in the company of strangers, they were all sitting, folding the newly-washed clothes and whispering God's news.

A white sheet, perhaps that of a wedding past, was dragged aside by the mother, my mother, in the hope that they, we, will be able to use it one day when she is no longer there.

XII

It looks like a horizontal line.

It is, in fact, a horizontal line which seems, from where I am standing, to be leaning on a rug of paper and graphite.

You bring yourself closer to it whenever you think you are on your own here.

You bring yourself a bit closer to that sound descending from the keyhole and its echo as it moves closer to its source.

You are too scared to look it in the eye while you constantly move towards it.

It is the same God that my two young nephews disagreed about in the camp when one of them drew a line claiming it to be vertical while the other, to this very minute and from where he is, remains certain that what he still sees is a horizontal line.

I can see neither. The God of asylum does not exist.

XIII

And the place is what enables me to be mad. Mad, but sane, or, one might say, a tad mad, a tad sane. Mad amongst my mad brothers whose bodies are neither mine nor theirs, I can say. I can also say that madness is the shadow of the place, the one thing that does not desert the place but comes and dies with it.

XIV

The wound can be seen from a distance like a well to the lost, the thirsty and the asylum seeker. Seek to feel it for it is yours after all. Will it be your body or the wound on this day - a normal day? The whole body is right here and right here there is only a wound.

XV

In silence, we foretell the end.

Fingerprinting

She did to me what a friend would normally do for a friend or a lover for another lover - she held my hand very tightly.

When I looked at her, my fingers were above the scanner - my flesh was scanned and so was the air around us.

I thought of looking her in the eye again, pretending that we were in love and in that room where asylum-seekers and suspects gather it was our opportunity to embrace one another while the machine was doing its job.

I gave my fingerprints and left.

Every time I think of that moment I feel the need to go back to that terminal and ask her what it meant to touch a stranger.

Her name

I held my mother's hand firmly as she was trying to write her name for the first time.

My hand clutched hers without realising that was a genuine and yet necessary demonstration of intimacy.

There was no eye contact between us.

The only thing we were both able to see was her slightly trembling and untidy name imprinted in graphite on the first page of my notebook.

My mother's feet

How would I not think of them when every being can see them as they drag themselves into the soil, the solid and dry soil of our house.

I would even say that they belong to me as much as they belong to her.

The cracks - those symmetrical and orderly beings - have always contributed to the way I see things, in a way that would even allow me to say that through them I can see a place that I cannot see.

The camp – is it possible?

When she gave birth to me, we bartered hands to caress time in time.

She says in the voice of the absent: Noise is the ornament and the story, and the sleeping thing at the threshold is for me despite me.

At the time my father was oiling his gun with the cooking oil gifted to us, a passer-by at the other end of the camp was killed by a stray bullet.

Two buckets, half full, and as many sheets ripped in haste from castaway things sufficed for us to cry together.

I am circumcised amongst the circumcised.

To recognise myself, I remember my body as I have never seen it.

My mother ululated the cut and cried the blood.

Is not circumcision in the camp a meaning for the future? Circumcision, what is it? The cut that is already cut. The curse in the flesh as pronounced by the sleeping and the mad. The flesh stared at before it is severed.

Does the cut not announce birth?

To become an utterance, memory survives the uttered.

For the sacrificial before sacrifice, we planted ourselves next to their scarecrows: faces for the arid…

I write the camp, memories as scattered as our rationed flour, in the congested veins of my mother as she pushes the seasonally borrowed cart towards our wide-open mouths, the once lived life dusted off, polished, for the written in memory.

The cut is the parchment for the afterlife.

According to her, my father did not cry, but to feign crying he drowned himself in our tears.

I saw it happening and amidst the ululating heads I continued peeping to spot the face.

Whoever gives birth in the camp, gives birth to the archive in the shape of flesh.

If what is happening is real, wait until you see them ravenously gnawing at their shadows.

The camp – is it possible?

Memory: the pulse as the future.

In remembering, the ordinary is content with the ordinary.

Photographs

For the promise of the posthumous, I shall remember:

The unconsented dead, completely dead

The midwife, withered, reproaching my mother for dying

My mad grandfather who remained behind as dead

My other grandfather submitting his name to himself in anticipation of death

The cruel grandmother dying of a stroke without any sun

The maternal grandmother as the third wife of the first grandfather

My father crying over his overripe vegetables

My mother reciting the Qur'an by heart, mispronouncing her heart

All huddled together, almost complete, in two separate photographs.

Single life

There shall be no camp to write for the camp.

My fidelity for it is my fidelity towards its name like a name, as a name.

I cite you, not hearing but a mucus-filled voice, treading at its own rhythm, lamenting the lived in silence, laughing off those who tricked us to believe in time.

I sit on the edge, to the right of the unseen.

Your chin now has its single life – an overgrowth of half-shaded lines, splintered hairs, the size of a raindrop splashing beyond its home.

Thus she bore me: blind, all-seeing of catastrophes.

For her: crying is wailing's gift. Whenever they wailed, the thing wailed for Man.

A soliloquy before time

I tremble. The hand in the hand, smothered, breathless, air in between.

I tremble. My body is a garment hewn from cut-out fabric cast on the road, never a coincidence, an offer for the coming tense.

Who is it, the one, the only one to see the road amidst severed faces on unknown bodies?

The journey, what is it? A desolate land, a roaring sea, a name of names?

There, is nowhere for me. There I killed my father to steal the name, to sail towards the wildest of screams and never return?

My name, they say, is that of a prophet, and my mother's, the silent hand on my shoulder, is holy wood for coffins and ships.

I tremble in the name of the name as I see my eyes trespassing in every void and flesh.

I see them in every road, skinned limbs, a dialect gasping for sense and air.

We walk, so we think, never in the absolute presence of one another, breathing the blindman's stick.

We walk with feet as heavy as fate, as light as bodies not remembering their bodies.

Each a petrified soul. Each a time.

Time

I

The secret
Creaking of hips while journeying
Faces of sand wrapped in thick cloaks
Dates from the Hereafter sealed in the far end of fruit
A glimpse of something

A blink of an eye
Then resurrection
Things they see with their eyes shut
Things they may recognise with their senses and
Edges
The severity of sleep
As they hallucinate
Then an awakening
It is the time of the tree of the unexpected
Befalling them
Stomping on arid routes like a raging beast
Ravaging the thing guarding all things
In a pale of doubts and amulets
It is far
Farther than the stitch of sound to itself

Is it not, then, the creation of farness?

II

They come
Laps devoid of night
(Perhaps time was absent or
Perhaps it was them in their unworn bodies)
They come or so they say
(When they sought what they desired
When they prodded their shadows to follow them)
They come in seconds
In a time saturated with clarity – a clear time
Now they have come
Let us invite them over
If they agree
We shall walk behind them
Towards their promised cheerfulness and
Land

III

A secret concealing nothing save the time of the road
They walk on a thread of dust
Or water
So as not to forget their intentions in the air
Another secret, it is
Or
   Digging
   Ploughing
   Shoving
   Not finding…

   A sighting without a mirror
   Urns of fresh metal and
Time

   A voice withers in throats of flesh and
   Dies
Time's secret is screaming
Calling
So hasten the slaughter
Hasten it, O stranger
Time is a feast
Feast's a sound hovering in sound
In the sublimity of sound

IV

They say:
We will be just like tomorrow
A river
A just river
In the beginning, as in the end, water
The river we cross with scale
And memory
(Silent was the time then)
Hands ominously gesturing at the symbol and
Nothing
(One nothing)
We shall lend the touch its touch again
The time to the kingdom of the thing
The White Ghoul
The plain under the river
Where is the river?
Where is it
Where is the water's witch
The followers of water?

V

Sounds fall deep in the belly
(A hole in the belly)
Wreathed by the sun's orbits
The moon as it is, motionless as though devoured
Eyes growing rounder until they see another moon
A moon
The shape of a bead on a stranger's forehead

Sounds fall
(They rattle in the belly)
Time weds the stranger's intentions and
Leaves

VI

They sit with incomplete books and psalms
With a grip of what they do not know
With an amulet the shape of a place
These are similar-different things
Mysteries in the clarity of mind
Clear, sometimes, in their absence

They say:
Clear, do not be
Nor be time by the sword
A heart is for the stranger
God, find time, never find it
Drag it in full time
If You enter

VII

When will they come, those strangers?

To write their return to nothing from nothing

From dusty borders and
Crushed wheat

From yesterday

From their broken veins

When will some of this happen?

Will they return for their
Crops
From the faces that remained
From their still faces

Where is the place?

Where is time?

VIII

Where is time?
And what happened to the wind to take them with her
Where is time at this time?
When it remains
When it dies
When it does not return even after a while
Listen
(They listen)
Listen to what is coming
Beyond what is called silence
Listen
(They listen)
Let time go back to where it was

The journey shall begin

Writing the camp

What makes a camp a camp? And what is the beginning of a camp if there is any? And do camps exist in order to die or exist forever?

Baddawi is my home camp, a small camp compared to other Palestinian camps in Lebanon. For many residents, it comprises two subcamps: the lower and the upper camps that converge at the old cemetery. As I was growing up, it was common for children to know their midwife. Ours, perhaps one of only two in the entire camp, was an elderly woman, who died tragically when a wall collapsed on top of her fragile body during a stormy day in the camp. The midwife was the woman who cut our umbilical cords and washed us for the first time. She lived by the main mosque – *Masjid al-Quds* – that overlooked the cemetery. She would always wait by the cemetery to stop those who she delivered on the way to school, to give them a kiss and remind them that she was the one who made them.

The camp is never the same albeit with roughly the same area. New faces, new dialects, narrower alleys, newly-constructed and ever-expanding thresholds and doorsteps, intertwined clothing lines and electrical cables, well-shielded balconies, little oxygen and impenetrable silences are all amassed in this space. The shibboleth has never been clearer and more poignant than it is now.

Refugees ask other refugees, who are we to come to you and who are you to come to us? Nobody answers. Palestinians, Syrians, Iraqis, Kurds share the camp, the same-different camp, the camp of a camp. They have all come to re-originate the beginning with their own hands and feet.

Now, in the camp, there are more mosques, more houses of God, while people continue to come and go, like the calls to prayer emanating at slightly varied times from all these mosques, supplementing, interrupting, transmuting, and augmenting the voice and the noise simultaneously.

Baddawi is a camp that lives and dies in our sight. It is destined to remain, not necessarily as itself, so long as time continues to be killed in its corners.

Refugees are dialectical beings

Only refugees can forever write the archive.
The camp owns the archive, not God.
For the archive not to fall apart, it weds the camp
unceremoniously.
The question of a camp archive is also the question of the
camp's survival beyond speech.
Circumcising the body can indicate the survival of the place.
Blessed are the pending places that are called camps.

My father, who passed his stick on to me, lied to us all:
I slaughtered your brother so you would grow sane and
sound.
My mother, always with the same knife, cuts herself and the
vegetables.
The eyes which live long are the ones whose sight is contin-
gent upon the unseen.

God's past is the road to the camp's archive.
We strangle it, from its loose ends, so we can breathe its air.
Without its death, the archive will never exist.
In whose name is the camp a place?
It is the truth and nothing else that for the camp to survive it
must kill itself.

The transience of the face in a place where faces are bare
signs of flesh can gather the intransience of the trace therein
in its multiple and untraced forms.

The unseen – that is the field that is there despite the eye – can only be seen by the hand. After all, the hand and not the eye, is the intimate part.

Green in the camp only belongs to the cemetery.
The veiled women crying at the grave are my mother and my sisters. Once, my mother wanted to bring the grave home with her.
In the solemnity of the place, faces fall like depleted birds.
In belonging to the camp, senses premeditate their senses.

The aridity of a camp presupposes the aridity of life.
The concrete is barely permanence. If you pay attention you will see the cracks in their souls.
At the farthest point in life – the point of no return – dialects become the superfluous of the body.
Camp (n): a residue in the shape of a crescent made of skin and nothing.

Time, when killed, has no mourners, only killers.
The camp has its own signature.
What it signs and countersigns is never the permanent.
The camp is what remains when the meadows of the instant desert us.

The foot without a trace is a god.
Those who are arriving at the threshold are not one of us. It will take them time to know who they are.
Nothing is as old as the archive that is yet to be written.

The archive is always written in the future. (After Derrida)
Were I in possession of an archive, I would bury it by my
side and let it overgrow, upon my skin and inside my pores.
The enmity in the archive is the enmity of the intimate. By
detailing the body, the archive loses its sight.
I am absent or deemed absent. The fingers that I am holding
before you, in your hand – a sullen hand – are mine and
nothing else.
I wish it were possible to write the camp without the self.
In the camp, we surrender the meaning of the camp in
advance.
The camp is the impossible martyr attributed to the meaning
of 'dying for'.
In the camp, going to the cemetery is going to the camp and
going to the camp is going to the cemetery.
In Baddawi, reaching the camp only occurs through the
cemetery.
Is the cemetery not another home, host and God?

In entering the camp, time becomes suspended between
dialects.
The dialect that survives is never a dialect.
The dialectical subtleties in the camp are also called silence.

For the dialect to become an archive, no utterance should be
uttered.
Who is the creator of dialects? Whose tongue is the
shibboleth?
The dialect is a spear of noises.
Ontologically, the dialect is a being in the shape of a knife.
Only dialects can spot the silent Other.

My cousins in Nahr Al-Bared camp have always defended their dialect to the extent of preserving it in their fists.

I used to be asked to raise my voice whenever I opened my mouth. As if voices were ethereal creatures with an ability to rise.

Voices are the earthliest of creatures. Not only do they wreak havoc on earth, they remain silent in death.

What is it that makes a dialect a knife?

Is the dialect not a mythology of the silent?

To exist in the singular means the death of the Other.

'Dialects' is not a plural; it is the anomaly of a condition that should have never been one.

A ladder to God is the green in the cemetery.

In the camp, deserting the camp means summoning the certainty of the certainty. To this day, nobody has ever managed not to return.

Only in the camp do dialects outlive their people.

The untranslatability of the camp... We write it on parchments of time evermore, so it remains intact as a spectre when it is no more.

The dialect that survives on its own is that of the dead.

Dialects when uttered become spectres of time.

For us to hear ourselves we sign the covenant of the dialect.

A dialect always has a face – disfigured, a face nonetheless.

Where is the mouth in the testimony?

Those who come to us are never themselves in the same way we are never ourselves. When dialects descend upon the camp, the camp wails and ululates at the same time. In the presence of dialects, nobody knows what to do but to listen to the penetrating noise of the coming.

Is the dialect not the unavowable Other?

Refugees are dialectical beings.

The camp is time

Who writes the camp and what is it that ought to be written in a time where the plurality of lives has traversed the place itself to become its own time.

How will the camp stare at itself in the coming time, look itself in the eye; the eye of time, the coming that is continually pending, but with a face — human or otherwise — that is defaced? The camp is a time more than it is a place. Upon and above its curves, time remembers its lapses to the extent that it is its time — the one whose time is one — that preys on a body that is yet to be born.

In crucifying time neither it nor we can recognise the crucified.

God, incinerate the camp save the dialect. God, incinerate the camp, save the dialect.

The incinerator of time is the camp.

What is it that makes a sight worth a sighting when the seer can use his eyes alone for an enormity that no eyes can actually see? Is it the camp or is it its time that should be returned to its body to reclaim its body as a dead thing with multiple previous lives and none.

I write for it knowing that this is the last time that I write for it, herein the time is last and the last, it may belong to a no-beginning-no-end, but what it definitely has is its camp. The camp is time and time is the camp.

The possessive is what possesses the guilt that transcends all guilt and yet co-exists with itself until it becomes an event in its own guilt. But is it, is it my camp?

What am I saying right now, in this specific instant and under the false impression that the camp is mine? I say that it is the autobiography of the camp that is autobiographising the camp, suspended in time it is, while we deliberate the impossibility of narration in that context. In order to think of narration, not necessarily its narration, we follow it discreetly in the shape of ash.

In time, the mask takes off its mask.

The foot that treads is also time.

In time, we impregnate time with its time.

Time gives birth to nothing. The nothing that is raging nearby is our only time.

Time, tell us where your private parts are?

In the camp, time is hung like threads of dried okra.

The camp is the reject of the reject par excellence

It bears multiple meanings, depending on how it is said.
For my mother, however, the meaning was clear enough to
be taken from my father's mouth to God's and vice versa;
without allowing it to pass through a limbo of any sort. They
would normally fight over the mundane, the most mundane
of the mundane, and those most mundane of things would
remind us all that our voices really did exist and if they
were to be given the opportunity to exercise noise again,
they would do so to their hearts' content. My mother would
become silent and to reiterate her silence she would only
request to be left alone and be allowed to see God's face.
Now, they are both old and frail; my father is still in the
company of his voice while the woman, that woman, is still
looking for her face and God's.

Once, I asked my mother: Mother, in the absence of a place,
who invites who? She looked at me and said with a
concerned tone of voice: My son has gone mad! Hurry!
Hurry up! Summon the imam to recite over him!

Madness is what accompanies us to the unpredictable, to the
camp. The camp's unpredictability lies only in the eyes of
the dwellers.

It is the tremor in the hand that invites. My grandmother,
in Nahr Al-Bared camp, used to squeeze our little hands
whenever we appeared at her doorstep and say: How did
you leave the camp? We never answered.

By intending to capture the face, the whole body becomes
hostage to intention.

In intention, the prevalent tense is the past.

We never listened to my mother and always insisted on swallowing the chewing gum thinking that it might, one day, become a balloon that would transfer us to God.

Is the memory of the camp not the camp?

Suddenly, our senile neighbour stuffed her memories in a plastic bag and left.

The abstract in the camp is the body.

In the bomb shelter in Baddawi camp, in complete darkness, my mother, to ensure we were by her side, would count us, not knowing that, most of the time, the children she was tapping and uttering the number of belonged to other families.

The man whose sister is also my sister once asked me: Who is older, God or the camp?

The camp has its own sky. When people shoot in the air in happiness and in despair it is to kill the bird that is never there.

My father who has persisted in writing since a young age has not published a single thing. In his beige room, with eyes trying to see, he showed me one of the magazines with a poem of his that bore somebody else's name.

We look at it to see what it is that is not ill.

The camp is the reject of the reject par excellence.

In mourning the refugee, we mourn God's intention in the absolute

We repeat the repeated so we can see our features more clearly, the face as it is, the cracks in their transcendental rawness and for once we might consent to what we will never see.

They rarely return – those pigeons. The piece of wood that was meant to scare off the pigeons and entice them to return to their home landed by my feet. Not knowing what to do with it, I shut my eyes and threw it back in the direction of God.

The name is the loneliest of things.

What is recited is the voice and not the text.

In my camp, women slap themselves in funerals to never let go of pain.

Who can see it to say: It is? Who has the eyes to say: It definitely is?

The eternal in the camp is the crack. The crack also invites.

What is a camp? Is it not a happening beyond time?

A camp, to survive its happening, must become almost a camp.

The sublime in the camp, what it is? Can it not be the camp gestating with its impossible meaning?

His feet were in water and the hands were by his side as flat as nothing. While the tea was brewing, he prodded his father's shoulder to ask about the number of graves he dug today.

Nothing can outlive Nothing when Nothing escapes not the idea of living, living like twigs left alone to decay under the sight of the mother tree.

Does the camp not have a gender?

What speaks in the camp is nothing but the foreskin.

These are not headscarves but heads forever wrapped in themselves.

In mourning the refugee, we mourn God's intention in the absolute.

A sudden utterance is the stranger

The moon is the birthmark of the refugee.

His birth equates to the mauling of his entire body.

Nothing is anomalous about the wound.

While waiting, we bite our nails and flesh.

Once I dreamt in God's language. In my extreme ecstasy, I swallowed my tongue.

A dialect is a circumcised lip.

A sudden utterance is the stranger.

Only when tongues age, do dialects become old enough to leave.

An utterance en route is the utterance that can never promise.

In the camp, measuring air by hand by no means connotes the intimate.

In the camp, directions are needles in time's back.

The camp, to sustain its body, shrinks its limbs.

The camp has its own God.

The spectator is whoever cannot see his face.

Death, to carry a meaning, carries its offspring.

The camp is the tomb that has yet to find its dead.

Could it not be that the tomb is the name?

Only the dead lead us to the cemetery.

Confessions

He alone could scribble something so obscure in my school report. I would look, eyes wide, at shapes as textured as the palm of his hands. Elongated things, criss-crossed roads, intentional or semi-intentional smudges, bruises, faint or otherwise, around, above, through and underneath his name, *Mustafa*; the chosen, the prophet, or just the name of someone who happened to know how to drag a pen across a small box, a space slightly bigger than a keyhole, usually a blue *Bic*, always counterfeit from the corner shop in my camp.

My mother would have her fingerprints taken at the gate of the UNRWA Distribution Centre, always in the company of a headscarf, wrinkly like the camp's chapped sky. I would say: Let me do it for you, to show you how a signature is born. A neat signature like that woman's lipstick, across the aisle, the one who only comes to us like a season at the end of the month. Or let me tell you a secret: my copying my father's signature, with a different name, a different time, in my friend's report pretending to be the father. The father who shot the three-legged stray dog in the head on a whim. I grafted my father's lines into whiteness, once, twice, ten times, until we both shouted: This almost looks like a signature.

The rations would be dragged from one end to another in a wheelbarrow. Flour, tins of tomato paste and corned beef, the occasional sardines, lentils, vegetable oil and ghee. Not pushed by me but by our neighbour's son, inked arms and shoulders, with illegible names and shapes, who would always pray in the last row to leave the mosque first to sell his rotting vegetables and what he steals from the rations to the outcoming worshippers. A trace of flour the wheelbarrow would leave from the Centre to the house – an amount, as my mother would say, that amounts to a day's worth of silent mouths.

Confession

To confess
to arrive in the past at God's doorstep
to know what was said, with a script's precision still lying on the tongue
to sign the past as a pact between God
and God

My Grandfather

Hallucinations or fallen olives and shadows
in once furrowed furrows
now transient dreams
Elapsed blossoms awaiting old footsteps
The omen of the few

Fragile is the language

The fragile field
The fragile ears of corn
The fragile eye
A wilting flower on a ruin
A summer and another summer that escaped time

A fragile heart
The fragile language

What remains of the camp when the name dies?

In the blink of the eye, its fleeting fluttering, the afternoon eyelid in its ghostly sleep. In bed, a mass of flesh, intervals of moans. Hair still veiled and still hair. Escaping greyness and air. Hands by her side, sulking, like sullen widows. Tablets for heart conditions and life seeping through the seam. Wrinkled memories tucked away. Some water in a plastic jug for the odd cough and the house plant. A small window with creaking hinges in the far end leading to life.

I return to see her guarding the threshold and the door, hesitant eyes, as quivering as the electrical cables in the camp.

The camp has its truth, the untruth of the dialect – the witness, the dissipation of all utterances, the battered pictures on its walls, the wailing with every death and every birth.

What we see in the camp will never be completely seen.

Only the past is active in Arabic.

To the camp we vow. To the camp and nothing else. With the severed right hand. With the limbs that were.

Are you the gods of time or the calves of fire?

On the edge of the camp are women, draped in black, bartering their time for a sighting of God.

My brother once saw the gravedigger sobbing over the broken handle of his shovel.

The dialect, wherein lies a camp.

The possessive, the intimate of no one?

The face that cannot see the face is its witness.

Witnessing and killing are analogous. Both acts betray silence in an attempt to live in the other's throat.

What remains of the camp when the name dies?

They burn reeds with reeds, and turn the sound to incense and incense to sound, and when the fire wanes on the slope, they rummage in the ash in search of sound.

Blindness is a guest. Leave it in your place and depart.

When he slapped me, because I stole water from the spring, he forgot that my tears are for me alone.

God is the water of time.

The eye sees only the pending.

The one who asked my sister her age became her husband. My sister still does not know his name.

The threshold which my father built with his own hands of stone and cement, grew, until it swallowed our house.

I caress my hand with my hand as I prepare myself for the war, the one, here and everywhere, that killed all of us and the air.

They said what they wanted to say before they left. As for us, their words did not linger long enough. It is somewhere near here, not far away, where they buried her. In this very spot there is still something like her but slightly absent.

I can no longer think. I can no longer feel my feet below me. And if you ever wonder what the matter is, just look and see what is before you.

They so desired dryness in that moment but it was never to be. They pulled them out one after the other. A wet pile waiting for the sun to reappear.

It's almost not a thing... – Nancy

Ibid. The bodies, the more or less intact bodies, were numbered. The lighter than the less light than the light...

That was the extra, the god who cannot accept to be displaced under any circumstances. The never-refugee.

We were escaping the air raid when my father spotted that fruit vendor selling half-price bananas. Not knowing that we were leaving a raging sky behind, he was so happy to find customers. There, all of us were sitting in darkness in the bomb shelter eating overripe bananas.

I did not see his face to say that he is no longer there. Or to lie to myself about what I have just seen.

For they were few, they wedded. They wedded each other at sunset. Now, before or after sunset, they hardly appear. Last time they were seen, they fell seriously ill.

It was the language that made him unwell. His stomach would churn and eventually vomit whenever they insisted on using it in front of him.

Abreast, breast to breast, and every other possibility. It is this, your and the other language, which makes me and us susceptible to betrayal.

As they were scanning his chest, the face suddenly fell off. (Maybe it was due to the impact of something; a thing, they said, in the air.) Using the bandages and the threads in front of them, they managed to put some back in its place. They patted it. One, two, three and a new face emerged in the open.

To depart at that moment in time, when dust and other particles are still on your feet, inside and out, and in the fine crevices, diagonal, and while every being in the vicinity, animate or otherwise, is roaming the place, not for a particular reason but for the place itself, would become the time that is already dead, the time that is forever feverish and never around. Then, when we have all departed, there will no longer be time for us to reach the place, the one place that we are still hearing about, to see it the way we see ourselves without falling ill again or becoming contagious.

It is here that I first saw it in its first self and it is here that I knew its name. In response, I moved a bit further away from it but made sure I was also here.

It says the name of the name. The name of all, everything and nothing. The name and more or less than the name and nothing else. This is what they have bestowed on me. The blessed ones. Because I remembered theirs, they granted me their name.

My mother treated them the way she would treat her god - she prayed to them day and night, but before coming near them she would wash herself in cold water and spray her headscarf with an unidentified scent. The ceiling was leaking and on that day the clouds were nearer to the place than ever. Since it was made of asbestos, repairing the roof was not an option. My father, the man of the house and the one who read Marx and wrote poetry in bed, would encourage her to go and beg the UNRWA people for a new roof.

My brother Ibrahim named him. He also made him follow us all whenever we decided to leave the place. Ibrahim in particular wept when my father and our one-eyed neighbour decided to castrate the sheep before dragging him to the slaughterhouse.

They were reciting their holy book or something like it. Their voices had a tenderness which was almost there. As we approached the door, they hurriedly descended to welcome us and inspect our faces. The youngest, or the only one who looked young, almost looked like me.

I am writing as the one, in close proximity to ritual, to those of you who never are. I am writing the text that I would like you to carry with you, on your soft backs, as you follow us and our movements thinking that you may one day see beyond our feet and their shadow.

There, we are building the place, a sudden place, so we can gather our thoughts and ourselves in the same place, so we can see the eye in front of us. We are waiting for you, as we wait for our footsteps by the door and at the door, waiting for what we cannot see with our naked eyes.

That is their flight, they said. That is their beast. But when will they meet Him and look Him in the eye? They are near. This is what they say. We have to believe them and believe what they say. They say what we believe. We believe them, so they say.

We are writing as the refugees of the place, the *khôra*, and since we are here, somewhere, somewhere in the somewhere, amidst you, we are here writing what we can see at once. This is not a prophecy, we have no prophets since they all died of their own causes at once, nor is it a text for you to believe in. It is, above all, what we have decided to carry with us en route; the route, a route as well, to you and to us. Barefoot we lie across time, not without feet, the same feet, but with extra ones, with and without flesh, veined albeit discreet, blue without any blueness, only the feet are still, the feet of time.

The religion that we will collect once we have time to gather, all of us, around the place, to summon one another from the forest, to create what will become the sound in the air: is that the place? Something is heard in the vicinity as though it were fleeing women nearing the abyss. Flee, we say. We hear nothing in return. They send us nothing save their sounds that become nothing. The religion that we will carry off the ground is theirs, we think; where they wash, recite and scream until they lose their feet. Not ours, but similar to ours. Not our mothers', but nearer to them than to their armpits. They do what we witness. They descend as we continue to see.

But what is our religion? Is there a religion after all when walking can only be measured by sweat? Is it the one, the one that chases us until we become afraid of ourselves? Or is it what they call numbness? It is everywhere like the ones who are still descending in the hope of finding their bodies. Or seeing the things that look like them whenever they find time to stop. This is the secret that we plan to strangle soon.

I arrived. I arrived at that particular time not knowing that was me. I arrived first and foremost, and to my own surprise, I have continued to arrive during this time.

I think of their language in order to die next to them. This does not mean that we will ever die together. Nor is it a statement of love. It is, above all, an attempt to stay silent.

The bird that has just flown off is my intention. From one branch to branch, a colder heart grows.

They called him forth. Nobody knew what he looked like.

My father used to lie to us when we asked him about our dialect.

He also lied about what he would do when the war stopped.

The bomb landed on our neighbour's roof. My mother was proud of us for keeping quiet and not screaming out loud.

At that time, nobody knew what was happening. It suffices to say that today has not happened.

There it is: the camp that is yet to be born

There it is: the camp that is yet to be born.

The camp's existence will always be on a par with time in the superfluity of tenses.

I do not know how the archive can become the soil's past.

The camp is also the pre-judgement of time.

Find me a place whose meaning is that of its absence.

Find me a place where nothing is not exactly nothing but its equivalent.

Religion in the camp is not one. It is the limbs, prosthetic or otherwise, that worship, not the body.

Can a ruin be a camp? When we dig, sooner or later, we dig the camp into the past that sees.

The thing, the thing that has no name but forever exists, is what a ruin is.

His cane, that which sees for him, is God's face despite itself.

Even to go for an outing, an outing from a camp to a camp, so short to the extent of not happening, for my mother, necessitates worrying about being left without a camp.

Home: the distant in the distant, the near in the near, wherever my mother departs, the soil and the metaphor sipping from the same dry well, what my grandmother calls the law, the cut in the hand and the tongue, the archive or the departing dream, the slaughtered neighbour, the hidden knife, my mother ripping off her dress and headscarf in sadness, the tree in the cemetery, the cemetery as a tree.

Necessarily, the camp is the border

There, the noise is also the religious.

On a day as chilly as the pulses of those who took away
our things and left the door ajar, you gave birth to me in
darkness: you, the midwife, two whitish towels patterned
with dry blood, and a bowl of hot water. I, to my utter
surprise, bore you from within, at once, with no pain. Now
I know why you used to call me 'my mother' whenever
I slipped away from my dialect and pretended I ate that
which you served me and my siblings, of the cracked wheat
you cooked. You said: Eat it. It's good for you. It's good for
your memory. You never said that was what was left of our
rations, of your undying walks to the distribution centres.
Mother, allow me in your absence, while shrouded in the
last sound of your sound, to call you: My mother. Mother,
listen carefully, mother: I am your mother.

When we entered, the path was nothingness and
nothingness was a path.

O Enterers, depart from yourselves to see in your naked eyes
the offspring of the border…

The worst of fates is not to arrive in your place.

The place, to protect itself, surrounds its limbs with spears.

Instead of wheat they grind their memories.

Nobody knows for sure a refugee's age.

The border is not bordered except by the coming death.

Only in the camp is the right age read through the hands.

In the archive everything begins and ends with the archive.

The archive whose writing is yet to happen is also called God.

Necessarily, the camp is the border.

We wait before the place never to claim the seen but to count the eyes of which we dream.

Come to the camp to remember what will never come.

The definite is the shadow and not the owner.

Those feet are the creator of time.

The camp will always remember its birth as the question of the question which never ceases to return to its body.

The singularity of the camp equates to the singularity of God whose existence is predicated on complete solitude.

The body of the camp is the bearer of time. When the camp outlives time it outlives itself for itself.

In other words, the camp is whatever is far from clarity but near itself.

Smells in the camp are the body proper. They arrive in advance of everything including the body.

Refugees to awaken themselves stomp their feet upon arrival.

The obscurity of what a camp is is the obscurity of language whenever confronted by its nothingness.

Even when it is approached, the word "camp" will always be held at the frontier.

We store our dialects in broken hearts in advance of death. Might we die without our dialects one day?

You sin. You recite verses upon which additions float. You say: The host is an addition. Your throat swells up as you squeeze words out of sounds and sounds out of words. You pray while water sweeps the intact point on your forehead. I enter with tentative feet. Past your mat tiptoeing: Verses, like running water, fall from above rapidly as though something were to happen. As though I were brothering the devil in my silent whispers and my father's spluttering in his room. You were hardly there, only a handful of words hanging from your long white dress.

The promise contains the promise.

When a promise is uttered, language dies.

A bird ploughing the air is the dialect.

In the camp, we can only see the camp's shadow.

Dialects, too, get pregnant.

What is still in the dialect is the name and nothing but the name.

Flesh when mutilated called God

Time is God's journey to his shadow.

An incomplete sentence is the place.

In the non-occurrence of birth, aborting the camp becomes the only possibility.

Might the dialects be the place that will be?

The hole is its hole, wailing and waiting for the green to sprout.

In a brass bowl with dangling rings as raw as young earlobes, my mother would pour us water whenever a plane broke the sound barrier, thinking that this would calm our fears and interrupt the deafening cries.

There, they interpret life as a sign of life, no more, no less. When their old wall collapsed, they erected another using their house plants.

In betraying the static, we narrate water with water.

What we pour on ourselves is also called narration.

The neighbour's tattoo inflicted by another neighbour still bears the faint name of another neighbour's daughter.

Sometimes I wonder how a god would look if he were to have my mother's broken veins.

A god with broken veins is a god who has ultimately given birth.

The Lebanese shopkeeper on the edge of the camp who used to buy our UNRWA tomato paste tins, once said: I was sorry to hear about your father's death. That was what my mother decided to tell the man to make him pay her on time.

The meaning of time is the meaning of what can and cannot move in time and at the same time.

The elderly woman by the mosque once claimed to have seen time in the flesh.

My camp's gravedigger neither prays nor fasts, he is only capable of digging.

Skinning is separating the skin from the flesh, never the flesh from the skin.

My mother tells me that the butcher who sells her meat still swears on his daughter's life that he slaughters his cows with his own hands.

The same butcher who still sells meat to my mother is, according to our distant relative who knew him from another camp, neither married nor does he have a daughter.

Eye, the orifice of oblivion, the camp is certainly before you.

Ageing in the camp is a rehearsal for ageing in heaven. Neither acts require proof to sustain their time.

Whose consciousness is more reliable: the animal that rarely kills or the man who rarely dies?

When the war ended, my father washed the blood off our threshold and gave us a bath.

And what shall we call a camp that is completely there?

The camp's genesis lies in its consciousness of itself.

My mother used to bake us bread and deliver it to school so we could eat, so we could stop looking with envy at our friends holding their bread filled with things. On that day, the school gate was closed but a hole was there. Desperate to reach us, my mother's hand got trapped clutching the bread. To this day, we do not know why my mother, to free her hand and alleviate the pain, did not let go of the bread.

The camp never ceases to exist. A place it is not, but time inhabited by time's selfishness.

Is it not the visceral which binds us to the camp? The feeling in its rawness which drags us to it – to a breast or a lap so dry, as fossilised as our time?

In our home, in the piles of books and notebooks left to their time, I spot my school book: half-faded letters, lines smudged by dampness and traces of rust, my name thinly written on its own on a line.

In total darkness, with no eyes to see me or faces to lament the non-presence of light, I held her hand tightly, thinking that, sooner or later, that light would be back and our eyes, open and shut, would once again return to guard our hands from our hands.

Nothing arrives in the camp. The neighbour with the prosthetic leg once said: I swear by God (pointing at the artificial limb), it feels like mine.

The camp is grasped in its absence.

To kill time, the camp sheds its innards.

The inhabited and the inhabitant share the same limbs. Once their sweat was the same. He would throw his jacket over the school wall so his brother would wear it after him. As siblings, their main arguments revolved around whose smell the jacket had kept.

My mother's hands, distant as they are, would intertwine, the right above the left, to press the devil back into her tummy and pronounce the end.

In writing the archive we submit to the perishable in writing.

Yet there is something to hold… The women in the long lines, above their invisible legs, outside the distribution centres, with hair hurriedly tied up underneath the headscarves, cannot write. In anticipation of their names being called and their thumbs inked, they would tread slowly holding their hands as if cradling premature babies.

The teacher, who asked me to swear by God three times that my father did pray when he handed me a sealed envelope with a bit of money collected by the school for the poor, did not know that my father never accepted that money but instead returned it to the mosque, claiming that he had just found it.

She would always insist on giving me some. In her hands, she would gently rub the dry mint to softness. From lightness, to falling shades, to lightness again. A sighting of sublime dissipation: the leaf, a fragile wing, becoming its own fragility.

The tree in your name, we will recite. The name chosen hurriedly by your father. You were barely a few hours old when he recited it to himself in front of curious strangers as a beginning for something which would never age to die or die to age. Then, neither of your parents knew how to read or write. It sufficed for them to utter the name for the name to be carried across the arid fields of May into the absolute. The letters are now long dead and the wailing, which has never ceased reverberating in those distant furrows, has come home.

What is it that is not a camp?

When the war ended and before leaving the bomb shelter, my mother asked us to check we had everything.

I am writing the fragment within me, the incompletion I behold as a sense.

In the camp the barest attachment to earth becomes the ultimate survival on earth.

A pending mourning in the name. A pending mourning is the name.

For the concrete in it, for what is there for it from times past, the monumental speaks. It speaks to itself, in its own voice, to what once was. In the hope of an ageless silence, it speaks – a silence which is as imperceptible as time.

There, whenever time comes, we cross from age to intention. We seize speech from behind our ears like overripe fruit, with care, and once caught we start again.

Flesh when mutilated called God.

In dying, flesh prefigures flesh.

As precise as the body is the wound.

On my uncle's floor, the one who sells second-hand clothes to his Lebanese neighbours, I shook my tooth until it fell out, to make a window like my mother's.

Crossing the threshold is to confess without speech.

In the camp, confessing occurs before knowing.

An avowal to an avowal is silence.

Tense as a tense, persuasive as a mask is the camp.

I once saw her imploring God to rid her of her husband while exposing her old breast to heaven.

In the camp, the foot which outlives the other is called a witness.

The bomb shelter

The bomb shelter:

The camp's alibi for a presence susceptible to its presence
The private parts of the dead, circumcised with hindsight
Guts as road signs   Or a map
Ruins summoning ruins   Ruins fornicating ruins

In rows, they ululated. The bomb shelter? The camp contracting to its essence.

The precarious is the non-existent. There, in the much deliberated existence, will always be a missing limb.

Who stayed behind to count the void that is?

A shelter to come and a camp that is.

In the canon of dust, the camp deprived of its shadow is a shelter.

Only dust departs and remains at once.

When they built it they carved its past out of God's shoulder.

In the consequence of time, the shoulder shall return to God as severed time.

The shelter's guardian who, to the best of my knowledge, was not Palestinian, had a lisp and around his discoloured neck was a chain with an empty bullet for decoration.

My son, anger not a stray bullet, remain in a place that was.

By shadowing its coming, the camp mimics the future.

The string my father used to pull his tooth out, as the bombs were falling, snapped in half. Two almost equal strings suspended in total darkness awaiting new blood.

Declare it even if God is certain of that which long passed. In good time, time cuts the throat of time.

A tomb for the hesitant. A wreath for men and metals…

No clouds for the face. Water for the tomb and the house plants.

In my naked eye: I saw my sister running away from a bomb, stark naked save her eyes.

The bomb shelter is one third of the camp. In the fraction, neither are not alone nor are they not together. A fractioned fraction, an escape route for stagnant intentions.

When we left the bomb shelter, our dusty faces stayed behind. Inside, is where we swapped faces in haste.

It is still war so no remembering to be remembered behind those walls

But the nests for the hovering metal

Outside, time is tomorrow

Or could it not be that which was not

It is still war according to their pulses

On their lips: God recites the eye

The pierced eye

Eyes to the extent of not seeing

The border as the dual

Outside place

The indifference to all beyond dying

The indifference to the indifferent death

To the binding in time

There is some time in waiting: the pail tentatively suspended from the handle. A dry well in the vicinity, feigning sound…

In the bomb shelter, I wet myself so I would mark my spot.

The wailing inside never ended to the extent of our dialect becoming wailing.

To repel the evil eye, my mother would only count us under her breath.

I cannot remember it all. What I can remember for certain is memory twisting our neighbour's neck.

Imminent are the whispers of time. Whenever it is whispered, it is whispered so they stop to catch their breath and stretch their legs.

The imminent never arrives. A contract between time and another time it is.

To make carrying the gun easier, the young fighter dressed his gun's arms with his mother's old socks.

Inside, the residual is always in the air.

The residual condemns all to waiting.

Inside the shelter no one ever asks about the time.

Time is the time of our excrements parted by unannounced ceasefires.

When the bullet punctured her lung she was squatting in the name of time.

No one survives time, not even God.

Violence! In your name, meaning shall kill itself.

A fistful of solitude

The face is dying, the face that sees everything but cannot see. The face that sees that it is dying so it can die. The face that is dead, not now, not later, but in the instant that precedes the above.

The *be* is there. And there is nothing as the head falls by the feet. It is the same head that was once attached to that tree. The head that keeps looking down to see what is about to become. The *be* is there, a stone's throw from the head and the tree.

It is my head and the head of the Other next to me. Can you not see death fast approaching?

The head is still the same, its own head, unsullied and fresh beyond belief.

It is my head that fell, and so did his eyes as they saw their dying.

The image that was still in the vicinity was as it should be, blurry, soundless and red.

That night I spoke with him. His face was rounder than mine and with only one eye to witness the encounter we decided, of our own volition, to look each other in the eye.

We will begin, as we are, both of us, with a fistful of solitude.

And if I were there, in their place, in their heads, I would adjust his slightly to the right without leaving a trace or causing any pain.

The prefix is above all a guest who betrays.

Is it distance or is it a far god?

I am seeing death. With piercing eyes, on a night as leaden as our other nights, I stare at the blade, the hand-sharpened blade, I once stole from underneath my mother's dream…

The rain that slipped like a stranger's love letter between a cloud and our neighbour's plastic pipe, is someone else's rain. At the feet of the tangled reeds along the riverbank is where we laid the place to rest and headed to nowhere.

I dreamt in your language. I dreamt of intention so bare.

The hand landed on my face, then a gushing voice. His interrupted evening and a cracked hand. So I should return the book, he said. The barely-scratched book I stole on my first day at school from her God-sent son with crooked legs and a silent voice.

I would carry twice my weight so I would sell my weight and return as myself. The camp was behind us and whenever my father and I remembered to breathe we would breathe out both of our weights into the air.

The lacking is the language and herein, on the side of my stuttering, is an amulet for loss – a loss in the shape of a language.

He bid his face farewell for the last time
with the swing's rope built on a rooftop for various thoughts
he wrapped himself.
He whispered
with the joy of the wounded with the wound in his imagination:

To those whose language I cannot speak
I submit my diary from a place I left in my dream where
all is slit by filed teeth and knives
If the air survived the hands

Gather the whereabouts of a voice in hessian bags –
bags as old as time

The dead's blood is not dead? In the bomb shelter, the woman, fading she was, combing her hair in front of a mirror and screaming children.

My mother's breast or the neighing of time?

I foresee. I foresee like my mother a thing climbing on the wall in the absence of earth. A thing yellowing, waiting for the rain in vain.

Under the cover of an eloquent darkness, in a stuttering present, below a metallic sky, I swallowed my language at once so I could give birth to her name and time.

At a time when time is a well-trodden land, I remember the camp, like a face, gazing at a shadow so deep in the flesh.

This time, scriptural, as narrow as the rooftops of a deserted camp, I say: When stillness was mine, time was. Time, the bastard of tales. Time, the innards of a beast, let me return to myself as soon as the camp is.

Can one write the trace?
The trace whose body is a trace
The trace that is before language and itself

When they brought me to their land, in a caravan the colour of my eyes, the fields as far as the eye can see were dewy... my mother's eyes.

It was at a definite time when their speech in time's sleep fathomed out a body for the disaster. Memories – then – became a sprig of grapes for a journey that was about to commence.

The fragment is patently plural.
A fragment for my mother's eyes

A fragment for her aged armpits
A fragment for the broken veins in her legs and my eyes
A fragment for the holy lack

There I faced my face and the camp that was. My brother was the driver. I was next to him. The car, in order to run, needed petrol, strong bangs on the engine and God's infinite words. He drove. He drove fast. I looked at him and the road. Sometimes, I looked at the road and him. He said: Can you see it? I said: Where? He said: Can you not see it? I said: Where?

When she appeared, I kissed her three times on both cheeks. My brother did the same. I looked around. I looked at her feet, bare and wet. As I was biting my thumbnail, the bit that was occupying me on the way, the coffee arrived. Followed by the sweets. Then the call to prayer. The men prayed in rows while the women kneaded and baked, and washed the new dishes. My aunt said: We can now see the sea and the mountains from here. The half-empty space was lying like a paralysed body in front of us. I said: And the cemetery? What about it? she said. I said: Nothing. She looked at us: Spend the night here. My brother said: Another time. My brother was the driver again and I was next to him.

I am to remain a claimant.
I admit my incoherence.
I state in the most direct terms that I am mad and that you are who you are.
I show you my scars to spy on your face.
I can see you before your eyes.
I lend you my hands and other limbs in secret.
I pretend to adjust my fingers to touch yours.
I talk and you listen.
I am god or so I am called.
I have my book and you have yours.
My number is a reference.
We are not different. We are not the same.
My name, my name, my name?

We are reciting the name of the camp so we can remember our names.

The visits we made were short. My mother would say: Never accept anything from your grandmother, her means are limited. While the blind man was reciting the Qur'an above the silent body, my mother's hand was hiding the few grey hairs that had grown in our absence on my grandmother's chin.

But what had vanished: Thing or Man? There we may say we are here until we are no more.

To spare your guts without knowing what is exactly there to be spared as they tell you in one voice: You have arrived. You open the car door and throw up everything in your already empty stomach on your bare feet. You throw up the water, the nothing that has been spared for this occasion. They lift your head and say to your face: The camp is no more and you are here to see what was a camp. You ask and ask about the names of those who are now neighbouring your dead and whether there is a chance that they might still be alive. The only answer that comes your way: Open your eyes further. Open them with all your might and see.

Is it distance or is it a far god?

The face?
That thing that never ceases to roam away from its body

In the green field on the border of a camp, the serenity of things sets a trap to time and other times. There, everything is amassed neatly: bodies, of similar cuts and faces, spare metal, unexploded bombs on the grass.

Then, the date was barely remembered. Nor was it ever inscribed save in the flesh. After some loud cries, my mother would drop us one after the other off her back, calling upon the divine to arrive at her broken veins and the fresh blood seeping on the concrete floor of our house.

This is my mother's blood.
The cloth does not absorb but the cloth.
As for the blood it possesses the perpetuity of nothing.
When the cloth fell, I saw pain for the first time.

Death is now. When they made their tombs higher, their intention was to hide themselves in death and life.

My mother walked before me. I followed her. With no eye contact or a breath, we stood side by side watching the tombs and the coming.

Will the camp ever become?

Sadness: a limbless secret.

The refugee or the camp will always see the other die.

It was the breathing that caught my eye. Every time we looked at them they pretended that their faces were not there. They would continue to move between the flattened houses, gesturing erratically, not knowing that they would walk past theirs without seeing it.

They planted what they once had in their previous lives. The pots were those of old ghee and powdered milk tins, rusty on the rim and with a few asymmetrical punctures, big enough for the water and air to seep through but never escape.

No pronoun can replace nothingness in its absence.

God of all, God of none.

The beating of the hand by the hand,
a vow of a vow from a void to another
so it would be content in itself,
the hand that was beaten to death by its other.

When my grandmother was laid in the coffin,
a green wooden coffin,
by many hands and sighs,
my brothers and I did what she did:
clutch our hands and wait.

I hereby or thereabout write what follows me,
the trace that is coming from all directions,
the unseen directions, in a language that is piercing through my
veins
like a beast with multiple heads.
Definite, miniature pores the skin has
and what is beneath the skin belongs only to the skin.
I stare at it and it stares at me wondering who the definite stranger
is.

The name always precedes the named.

Nothing but the name knows God. If God is the name, it is
for God to decide whose name it is.

Camp, arise!
Arise from spectres —
from a place that had carried you to a place when time was barely
time.
Arise now to return to a pasture of voices — faint voices and cries,
to the glorious cemetery and its dead, to the death whose death has
never been.
Arise to become the crucifix of sight,
the metal of all metal.

I am looking at my mother's back. I am looking at her from
behind, crying her eyes out at her mother's grave – a wilting
spine like God's first tree.

I am inviting you and myself in the name of the continuous
that has barely seen its face but run away from it. The invitee
or otherwise I am, with or without myself by my side, or a
place to become, I stand at the gate of the camp looking at
my shadow and the strangers ascending, clutching nothing

but my empty hands and a number. I say: You will arrive in a place that belongs to no one— a place as distant as a metaphor in His well. You will arrive as a guest and nothing else, with an intact body and two complete hands: to the body is one and one to the place you may see. I am inviting you and myself in a tense that belongs to no one save its tense and tension.

This incurvate male in the instant before departure
The multiply-awakened female from a chain of serenity
Another gender
Look at time (the time of the end)
A journey of feet made of water
A journey telling the trace without a trace
The refugee: a doer and land
The refugee: a river of tales fenced in by the dead's texts
Whoever survives, survives alone

The mother before time is still weeping and
God in the great book scatters his signs and time
On the empty pavements
Will you die? Asks the voice.
Will you die?
Will you die? Repeats its echo.

The coming is a coming gender
The coming is a fit for the total past

The secret's death is a secret.
Salt a neighbour?
Flies hovering on the soaked wood
What will remain are words for dying

The refugee:
Whoever comes without a language.

In the severity of place, nothing remains save a lonely deity.

An infinite outing; or the cemetery

As we walk, we remember: memories to me and the equivalent to her. We remember that those who watch are the ones whose traces are prior to their essence. They live. They die at the same time, to the extent that contracts are exchanged hastily, amongst themselves. They utter the same words in the name of the same thing. No time to revere the unseen. No time to lament the superfluous in sand. A camp, it is, sufficient in death as it is sufficient in itself not being a place to place.

To my mother, it is through the old cemetery that women can reach the cheapest greengrocer, he of the roaming eyes and no sons.

Before we set off to the cemetery to see who will be there, we leave our intentions in the distance: a few hundred metres from where the house is, the house that is named after the eldest son by an unsigned covenant between the father and the son, to stipulate the name in its name and to name the house so it would be its own memory.

Shoelaces are tightly tied and the feet inside these things are readying themselves for the untrodden.

When will questions disappear in living when living can be (to them) an orderly walk from life to death through a place?

She says: The cemetery is feminine. She adds: But all things; the place, the camp, time, are not. The road is in-between.

My mother repeats her dead mother's words: Do not lean on the wall, the neighbour's slaughtered chickens' blood is still fresh in our veins.

The splattered blood is all from the neck. Is it not the neck that is cut but lives on for exactly the time that takes time to become past?

They ask in a voice barely leaving their dry mouths: Why the camera? Why is the scandal happening before us?

Could it be to capture time on its deathbed?

To become an event, beside its event, the eye before the thing should be captured. In the captured, nothing has a date.

The hostage. The host in her time.

Herein, life dwells in the neck of the future. Like a knife, a knife that kills, a knife that lives.

What is there to be walked?

We shall see the photograph as it will be; in the face's repulsion from the seen, an unannounced touching, a coincidence for an embrace before its departure.

The face. Also the scandal as it recurs on the edges of the benign.

The worthiness of being sighted in the worthiness of a prosthetic limb.

In the cemetery, above the tomb, not too high from the graspable, in the company of time and with it. An instant's embrace, initiated by no one. Elation for a transient promise. The excess of a smile.

We must dig, day and night, dig the buried thing out, to see its happening in its non-happening.

In the camp cemetery there is no coincidence but the place.

In this place which is deracinated from all sense, all are equal.

Could it be that only death is sovereign?

Death's opposite is far from life. This life, as it tilts towards the vanishing, does so within its means. Is it not the vanishing, the ruin in anticipation?

Those who come to the cemetery are the dead, not as much as death itself but in accord with what is not dead.

In the ordinary, things hail their things.

By hand, by her clean morning hand, they woke up to her death. No one's guilt, they said, but the hand's. To forget, they mind the daily: beating the rug to make dust, tracing a leak in their hearts, waiting for time to make contact…

Sensitivity

In that empty reservoir cemented by my father I once hid hoping that at a certain stage I would drown alongside my image.

Imbalance

Translating one's name into another environment can make the actual name less valid.

It was early morning, the day that we all got up roughly at the same time, to realise that it was different now and we should no longer await my mother to bathe us one after the other.

We should, instead, accept that we are all grown-ups and responsible for exposing our bodies to ourselves without being committedly battered by my mother's sponge.

I recall the moment I stood up in that narrow place, for the first time on my own, unable to carry my weight.

Seeing

Between seeing a speck of dust and your hand is a line of argumentation that ends as soon as it begins.

You move your eyes from one object to another to kill time or observe what cannot be contained at that moment.

You sit and observe that which is not going to appear again.

Seeing things is bidding farewell to the mobile and the static simultaneously.

Dialects

I would say that my father has a dialect and so does my mother, but we have unknowingly and unhurriedly developed a new one.

That, to a large extent, was our dialectal revolt against my parents' dialects and, to a lesser extent, it was an announced verbal move against the inherent fixation on the so-called *authentic.*

At secondary school, one teacher in particular never liked my dialect since it did not, according to him, convey enough Palestinianness.

I was sad and, not knowing what to say to the headmaster, I decided to lodge a complaint against the teacher.

The main reason, as it was recorded then, was that the teacher was obsessed with his own purities; an obsession that so explicitly corresponded with his unwillingness to see or hear a dialect other than his.

Face

It is where we direct our faces to then say: We may have
been there.

The throne

No one has ever seen the bereaved mother. They arrived at night bearing nothing but their cries.

The father, the son, the wheelchair.

The order is merely an aesthetic thing. Or more precisely an echo of the bare survival of the extremities and the fall of the middle, the disabled middle, the son, who was brought from Aleppo to die in the camp.

(A fistful of absence suffices for the absent ones).

The father could not surrender the chair after surrendering the son to his death, but to ensure it stays in its place he tied it tightly to the window railing.

Like The Throne Verse hung in my mother's room, the chair appears suspended between what is yet to be inscribed in time and the chiasm, a tilting crucifix.

It is a camp despite the name

Existence, as it is, happens in the intentions of things.

A sign or signs piled on top of one another, barely separated by air and the narrowest of voids: white on blue or blue on white. There is a background – an undercoat – and then the words. But which is which? On the sign are arrows pointing to places, including to Baddawi camp. Names of old and new places neatly and orderly enclosed in this rectangular space. Positioned then adjusted to be made more visible to passersby and cars alike.

It is the Baddawi slope. The road that leads to everywhere and nowhere. The exact road which gave us and my mother trepidations as she stopped taxis on the main road going to Nahr Al-Bared camp. We would, upon my mother's prodding, hide behind her. Most of the time seven little bodies clutching her dress, looking for a handful of cloth, most of the time ending up inadvertently clutching each others' hands. The taxi driver would normally drive off the moment my mother would start asking him for a discounted fee: 'They are little, treat them as one. All of them on one seat and myself on another.'

My mother, to secure a ride that does not go beyond our limited financial means, would contract us into one: one body made of seven heads like a mythical creature who only grows in the camp. Many self-subtracted to one.

The sign is new or at least it previously was not there. The first sign to point to "Baddawi camp" alongside other places. The first sign to have the word 'camp' within its folds – a piece of evidence to the existence of the camp. To the presence of a place whose name is validated by a correspondence, a genitive one, between the proper 'Baddawi' and the noun 'camp' and yet it is the latter which is always remembered. It is a camp despite the name.

With a third eye, I see the catastrophe

[I write the secret].

On the doorstep, finding her way to the seeds that escaped her lap: Like the one who read the book, Son, read my swollen legs, another's land.

The camp happens in the distance.

With their permission, they disappear. With their permission, they return in hiding.

Ruins endure ruins.

Humming: the well is in the well.

Mother: There is no longer time, and the concealed in its place is its road to the thing. These days, her days are strange. The evenings are stranger. From the uttered to its evidence, she loosens the cross's crux to hang her headscarf.

The disease is not yet here. Alongside our heavy hearts, we have what will be: flour, beads of yeast, whole and crushed lentils, potatoes, their red soil to nurture escaping blessings in dryness.

I do not follow he who thinks well of time.

I grew old and the camp before me is the purest of ageing.

The father, late in his imagination, is also the infinite gratitude to death's eloquence in prioritising the prioritised.

In the camp, we arrive not. Nor do we remain. In ailment we only remember ailment.

With blessings without name, they resume wailing, each from the throat and all from the camp.

An ailment – as though it were a mouth inside a mouth.

What does a disease have for us to die?

Hastening death does in no means suffice to repel death from the face. Whoever will die in this instant, is already dead, but for death to survive interpretations it delays its own.

I repeat: Cursed is the complete in the flesh.

Camp, awake! Not for the innate deafness in the voice. Awake to see with the eyes of dust the effect of killing in time.

Certain we are in this death, that the sun will never be for us, to see the enormous death.

In this time we remember those who are long gone, not those who will certainly die. In darkness, memory looks at its feet.

Who will inherit the disease in a place that was in the beginning a place?

When the camp falls ill, tomorrow falls ill for its sins.

By tomorrow, by its disavowed promise, we promise the disease what we have of wishes: a camp big enough for death, a camp with fewer deaths.

He who is hardly awake shaves no more. The mirror with severed edges, bartered in shards between the sons, those perched over the shoulders of the almost identical curses, has a new line. From my old grandmother's mirror, the mirror of her beech closet, the one she bought in the city for the camp, my father in his spare time made us bespoke mirrors for our escaping faces.

As we wait for the disease, in echoless rooms, doors locked up, shutters dusted, thrust to the heart… The disease that will sign a pact with our diseases. In patience bereft of patience, we stand still behind our walls: without seeing, we shall see the disease that will be.

To my parents: When this is over, leave the dusk incomplete in its time and return, with fewer limbs, to your non-existent pastures.

With a third eye, I see the catastrophe.

Acknowledgements

I am indebted to the editors of the following journals, magazines, books and online fora where some of these poems – or versions of them – first appeared: *Asymptote*; *Critical Quarterly*; *GeoHumanities*; *Humanities*; *Modern Poetry in Translation* (MPT); *The Oxonian Review*; *Stand*; *Refuge in a Moving World; Refugee Hosts*; and *Refugee Imaginaries*.

I am grateful to the following people, projects and institutions for commissioning a number of these poems: 'A soliloquy before time' and 'Time' were written to be set to music, commissioned by Christopher Kent and Gamal Khamis for their narrative recital *Odyssey—Words and Music of Finding Home,* which was first performed in London in 2019. 'In arrival, feet flutter like dying birds' was commissioned for exhibition as part of the 2017 Venice Biennale Tunisian Pavilion. 'In mourning the refugee, we mourn god's intention in the absolute,' and 'The camp is the reject of the reject par excellence' were respectively commissioned and first published by *MOAS* and *Interruptions: New Perspectives on Migration*.

The AHRC- and ESRC-funded *Refugee Hosts* research project commissioned and hosted, amongst other poems included in this collection: 'Writing the camp,' 'Refugees are dialectical beings,' 'The camp is time,' and 'With a third eye, I see the catastrophe.' 'The throne' and 'It is a camp despite the name' appeared as part of the project's poem cards. 'The bomb shelter,' 'An infinite outing; or the cemetery' and 'Is it distance or is it a far god?' were commissioned by the AHRC-funded *Imagining Futures through Un/Archived Pasts* research project.

Sincere thanks to all who have supported and engaged with my work, especially: Amal de Chickera; Anna Rowlands; Bernard O'Donoghue; Elena Fiddian-Qasmiyeh; Elena Isayev; Homi K. Bhabha; Jamie McKendrick; Jenny Holzer; Kate McLoughlin; Lyndsey Stonebridge; Marina Warner; Matthew Reynolds; Mohamed-Salah Omri; Mohammad Qasmiyeh; Niall Paulin; Saiful Huq Omi; Sasha Dugdale; Subha Mukherji; Tamar Garb; Theophilus Kwek; Tom Paulin; Vahni Capildeo; Wen-Chin Ouyang; and Xon de Ros. I am particularly grateful to Aaron Kent and Broken Sleep Books for publishing this collection.

This work is for Bissan-Maria Fiddian-Qasmiyeh, Elena Fiddian-Qasmiyeh and for my family in Baddawi Camp.

LAY OUT YOUR UNREST